A Things to Make and Do Book

FRANKLIN WATTS | New York | London | 1979

Things To Make and Do for George Washington's Birthday

by Michael Cooper

To Crede Merchant

Library of Congress Cataloging in Publication Data

Cooper, Michael,
  Things to make and do for George Washington's
  birthday.

  (A Things to make and do book)
  SUMMARY: A collection of games, recipes, and
craft projects suitable for George Washington's
birthday celebrations. Includes a brief account of
Washington's life.
  1. Handicraft — Juvenile literature. 2. Cookery —
Juvenile literature. 3. Games — Juvenile literature.
4. Washington, George, Pres. U.S., 1732-1799 —
Juvenile literature. 5. Presidents — United States —
Biography — Juvenile literature. 6. Washington's
Birthday — Juvenile literature. [1. Washington's
Birthday. 2. Handicraft. 3. Washington, George,
Pres. U.S., 1732-1799. 4. Presidents] I. Title.
TT160.C67   745.59'41   78-11709
ISBN 0-531-02294-3

Almost everybody celebrates George Washington's Birthday.

It wasn't always that way. Back in 1732 when he was born, only his parents celebrated.

But soon George Washington grew up. He became a general and led the country's fight for independence. His soldiers celebrated his birthday then.

After the war, in 1789 Washington became the first president. Then everybody celebrated his birthday each year. All day long, people would come to wish him a happy birthday.

One way you can celebrate George
Washington's Birthday is to look for
a picture of him.

Which one is George Washington?

Where else could you find a picture
of George Washington?

You might find it
on some stamps,

or in a history book,

or on a quarter.

Can you think of other places
where you might find a picture
of George Washington?

Making a holiday greeting card is another
good way to celebrate Washington's Birthday.
And you can give it to your parents or to
a friend when you are done.

You need:

White Paper
Crayons

How to do it:

1. Fold the sheet of paper in half.

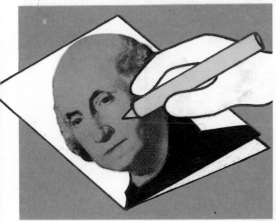

2. On the front of the folded sheet use your crayons to draw a patriotic picture. You might draw a flag, or an eagle, or a picture of George Washington himself.

3. Open up the sheet of paper. On the right side print the words HAPPY GEORGE WASHINGTON'S BIRTHDAY.

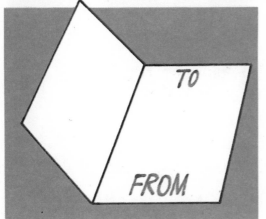

4. Now decide who will be the lucky person to get your George Washington's Birthday greeting card. Write his or her name above the greeting. Then sign your name at the bottom of the card.

When George Washington was a boy, the legend goes, he cut down his father's cherry tree. When Mr. Washington asked who had done it, George admitted he had. "I cannot tell a lie," he said.

Though this is not a true story, the cherry tree still reminds us of George Washington and his honesty. So let's celebrate his birthday by making delicious cherry delights.

You need:

Package of tart-size shells made of graham cracker crust
Can of cherry pie filling
1 cup of heavy cream
2 teaspoons of sugar
Tablespoon
Teaspoon
Eggbeater
Small mixing bowl

How to do it:

1. Put about two table-spoons of cherry pie filling into each tart shell.

2. Pour the cream into the small mixing bowl.

3. Whip the cream with the eggbeater until it starts to thicken.

4. When the cream is thick but not yet stiff, add the sugar.

5. Now, whip it some more.

6. Put a tablespoon of whipped cream on top of the cherry filling in each tart shell.

What a tasty way to remember George Washington on his birthday!

One of the finest honors to our first president is the Washington Monument. It stands 555 feet high and took 36 years to build.

You can make a small model of it in a lot less time.

You need:

An 8-by-11-inch piece of sturdy white paper or
  lightweight cardboard
An 8-by-11-inch piece of green construction paper
Ruler
Scissors
Pencil
Tape

How to do it:

1. Using your ruler and pencil, divide the paper into four rectangles measuring 2 inches by 9 inches.

2. Draw a triangle 2 inches high at the top of each rectangle.

3. Cut away the extra paper around the triangles at the top.

4. Draw two small squares in the middle of each triangle. These are the windows of the monument.

5. Turn the window side face down and make a fold along the side of each rectangle.

6. Next, fold the bottom edge of each triangle toward you.

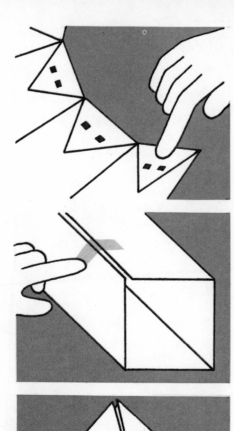

7. Join the two long edges of the rectangles together and fasten them with pieces of tape.

8. Now, bring the edges of the triangles together and fasten them with very small pieces of tape.

9. With your scissors trim around the corners of the piece of green paper to give it a rounded shape.

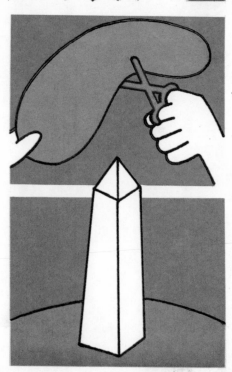

10. Tape the model you have made of the Washington Monument to the green paper, and the monument will look as if it is standing on a plot of grass.

When George Washington became the
first president of the United States,
he took the oath of office in New
York City.

That was the capital of the
country then.

People marched and cheered and
waved flags.

Flags were made by hand then because there were no sewing machines. But they were simpler to make at that time. There were only 13 stars. Today the American flag has 50 stars.

You can make your own 13-star flag to wave on George Washington's Birthday.

You need:

A large piece of white paper cut into three pieces—
   6½ by 8 inches, 3½ by 4 inches, 3½ by 11 inches
Blue and red felt tip pens
13 silver paste-on stars
Scissors
Pencil
Ruler
Tape
Glue

How to do it:

1. Take your 6½-by-8-inch piece of paper and using ruler and pencil, mark off 13 stripes, each ½-inch wide.

2. With your red pen fill in the stripe across the top of the paper. Leave the next stripe white. Color the next one red. Keep doing this until you get to the bottom edge of the paper. You will have seven red stripes and six white stripes.

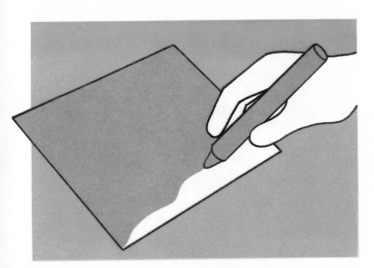

3. Take your 3½-by-4-inch piece of paper and color one side of it completely blue.

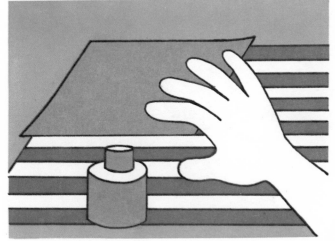

4. Glue the blue piece of paper on top of the red and white striped paper, putting it in the upper left corner.

5. Paste the 13 stars in a circle on the blue rectangle. The silver will look almost white against the blue.

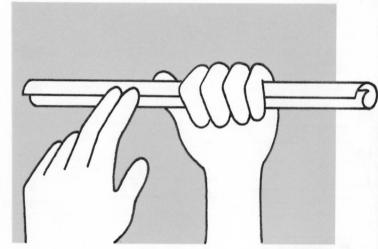

6. Now take your 3½-by-11-inch piece of paper and roll it into a long, thin tube. Fasten it with tape to keep it from unrolling.

7. Then attach the flag to the tube with tape. The lower part of the tube makes a sturdy handle so you can wave the flag.

In Washington's time men wore three-cornered hats, or tricorns. A gentleman wasn't well dressed unless he had one.

You can have one, too.

You need:

Paper
Scissors
Crayons
Tape

How to do it:

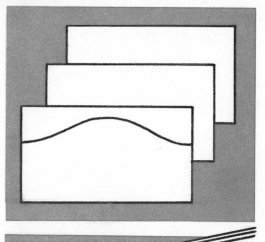

1. Cut out three paper rectangles, each about 8½ inches by 5 inches. Draw a curved line across one rectangle as shown in the picture.

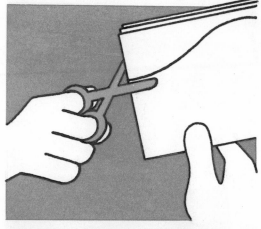

2. With that one on top, hold the three pieces together and cut along the curve with your scissors.

3. This will give you three shapes of the same size. Color them dark blue or brown, with a yellow stripe along the curve.

4. Tape the ends together to form a triangle, and you'll have a three-cornered hat!

What's in a Name?

You can play this game with the 16 letters in the name GEORGE WASHINGTON.

You Need:

Paper
Crayon or pencil
Scissors

How to do it:

1. Cut out 16 pieces of paper. They can be any size as long as they're all the same size.
2. Write each letter of his name on a separate square.
3. To play, everyone takes a turn and moves the letters around to make a word.
4. Somebody keeps a list of words as you go along.

There are many words

like *eggs*

and *shoe*

and *ring.*

You can make lots of words.
What are some of them?
Who will have the last word?

You will find more words on page 48.

George Washington's name is somewhere in this picture. Can you find it?

The answers are on page 48.

Did you know that . . .

George Washington didn't live in the White House. It had not been completely built yet.

Washington was the first to make Thanksgiving an official holiday.

WASHINGTON
STREET

There are 32 counties, 121 post offices, and over a thousand streets named after Washington.

Washington, D.C.,
our nation's capital,
used to be farmland.

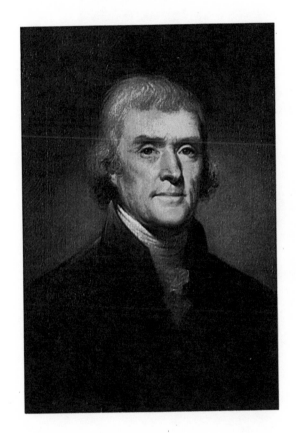

When Thomas Jefferson was
president, he would not celebrate
Washington's Birthday.

Each year more than
a million people visit
George Washington's
home at Mount Vernon,
Virginia.

During the Revolutionary War, Washington and his soldiers faced a bitter winter at Valley Forge. It was very cold, and there was little food — sometimes only oats and milk. But they always lit a fire and cooked what there was.

Valley Forge Oatmeal was simple to make. Today, by adding some special ingredients, it can be a delicious treat, too.

To make 4 servings, you need:

1½ cups of rolled oats
3 cups of water
½ teaspoon of salt
4 pats of butter
honey
raisins
2 cups of milk

cinnamon
a stove (and someone
   to help you with it)
a pot
spoons
4 cereal bowls

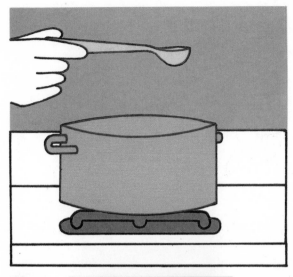

How to do it:

1. Add half a teaspoon of salt to the three cups of water in the pot and bring to a boil.

2. Stir in the rolled oats, gradually, so the water continues to boil.

3. Reduce heat.

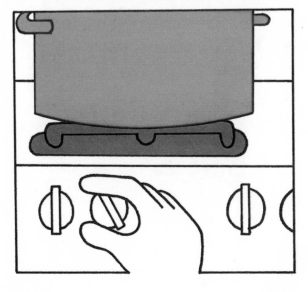

4. Add one handful of raisins.

5. Let it simmer for 10 to 15 minutes. Stir now and then.

6. Pour the mixture into the four cereal bowls and top each with a pat of butter.

7. Mix in a teaspoon of honey in each bowl.

8. Add a little milk to each bowl.

9. Sprinkle some cinnamon on top and enjoy!
It's also a good way to keep warm!

There are many ways to celebrate
George Washington's Birthday.

You can cheer him on his birthday.
A cheer is a kind of glad shout for
someone.

This one was written especially for George Washington when he was president. They cheered these words at a birthday party in his honor:

FILL THE GLASSES TO THE BRINK,
TO WASHINGTON'S HEALTH WE'LL DRINK,
'TIS HIS BIRTHDAY!
GLORIOUS DEEDS HE HAS DONE,
BY HIM OUR CAUSE IS WON,
LONG LIVE GREAT WASHINGTON!

You can salute Washington the same way with the same cheer.

Many things have changed since
George Washington was president.

Can you find all the things in this picture that were not here in Washington's time?

The answers are on page 48.

There were no ball point pens in George Washington's day. There were no fountain pens or felt tip pens either. People had to write with feathers. These were called quill pens.

Quill pens are fun to write with. You can make one. Almost any kind of stiff feather will work. Many flower stores sell peacock feathers.

You need:

A stiff feather
Bottle of ink
Paper

How to do it:

1. Dip the point of the quill into the ink. You need only a drop of ink at the very tip. Too much ink on the point will make a blot on the paper.

2. The pen can hold only a little ink at a time, so write until the point is dry. Then dip it again and write some more. It's best to go slowly.

Riddles and Puzzles and a Tongue Twister

Why are statues of
Washington always standing?

What's the best thing to
put into a George Washington
birthday cake?

What famous bridge
is named after
George Washington?

Why did Washington cross the Delaware?

What's wrong with this picture of George Washington?

How fast can you say:

Washington and his
weary warriors
whistled as they went
on winning the war.

The answers are on page 48.

Washington is known as the Father of Our Country, because he guided America through its early years.

The country was much smaller then.
There were only 13 states.

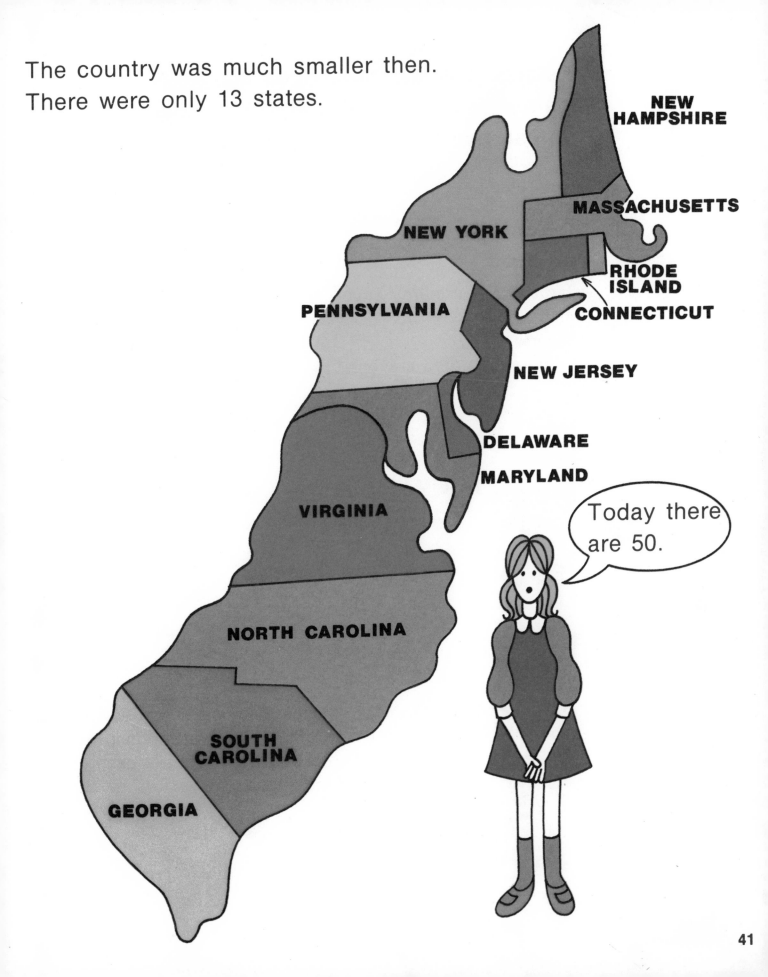

The map on page 41 shows how the 13 states looked. The shapes fit together like pieces of a jigsaw puzzle. You can make your own map puzzle.

You need:

A large sheet of sturdy paper
Pencil
Scissors
13 different colored crayons

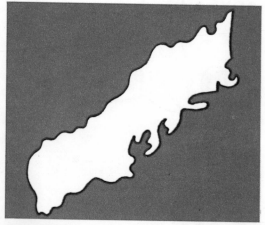

How to do it:

1. Draw an outline of the country on a sheet of paper.

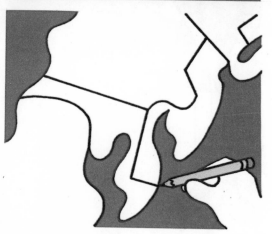

2. Draw the state lines. Remember that some states are bigger than others. Look at the map on page 41 again to be sure you make each state the right size and shape.

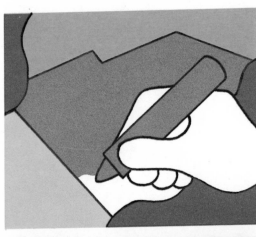

3. Crayon each state a different color.

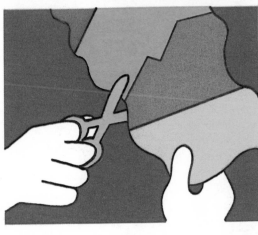

4. Next, cut out each state along its border.

5. Write the name on the back of each one.

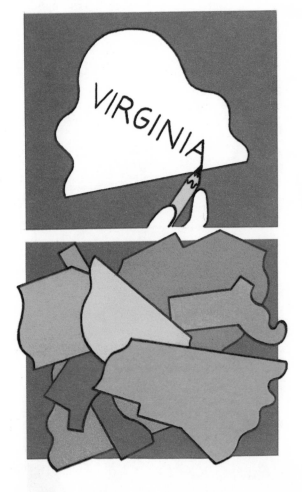

6. You should have the country in 13 pieces. How fast can you fit the puzzle back together?

Martha Washington was George Washington's wife. She was our first First Lady. You can honor her by planting a Martha Washington geranium.

You need:

Martha Washington geranium seeds
Potting soil
Pebbles or gravel
A 5- or 6-inch clay pot
Watering can

How to do it:

1. Put a half-inch layer of pebbles or gravel in the bottom of the pot.
2. Fill the pot three-quarters full with soil.
3. Put several geranium seeds on top of the soil.
4. Cover the seeds with another half-inch of soil.
5. Water the soil and put the pot in a warm place with plenty of sun. Geraniums need warmth and light.
6. Water the soil regularly, but be sure the soil has time to dry before you water it the next time.
7. Give the plant good care, and be patient. In three or four months you will see one or more shoots coming up through the soil. Soon after you'll have a plant with stems and leaves. And later on you'll have beautiful flowers as well.

Make a George Washington Picture Story

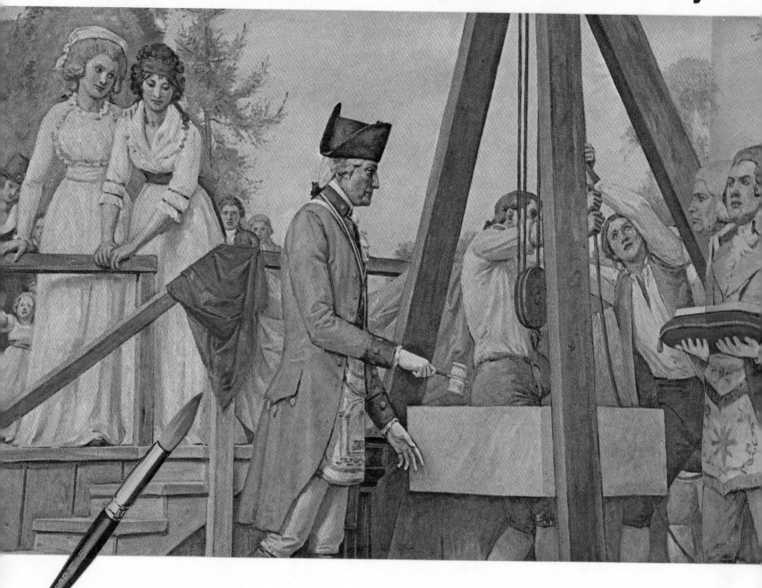

George Washington's life was filled with adventure and history. Many artists have made pictures of the important events. You can, too.

You need:

Old magazines
Paper
Crayons
Scissors
Glue

How to do it:

1. Imagine a scene from Washington's time. There are many to choose from. Each person can make his or her own, or everyone can work together on one big picture.

2. Look through some old magazines for things you might want to put in your picture about George Washington. You can cut out parts of pictures — clouds, or trees, or old houses, or even people's faces.

3. When you have four or five pieces cut out, start to arrange them in a scene. Do this on a sheet of white paper, and glue each piece in place.

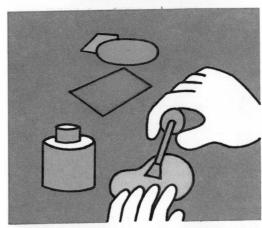

4. Now draw the rest of the picture with crayons. You can combine magazine pictures and your own drawing to make a picture story celebrating George Washington's Birthday.

Answers to the word game on page 24:

Wash	Was	Wheat	Ant
Go	Nose	Hog	Get
Sting	Sit	Wing	(and lots
Ton	New	Hose	more than
Snow	Gas	Want	can be
Went	Hen	Great	listed here)

Answer to find George
Washington's name on page 25:

Answers to the picture puzzle
on pages 34 and 35:

Factory	Electric lamp
Automobile	Television
Airplane	Telephone

Answers to the riddles
on pages 38 and 39:

Statues of Washington are always standing because
  he could never lie!
The best thing to put into a birthday cake for
  George Washington is your teeth!
The George Washington Bridge is named after
  George Washington!
Washington crossed the Delaware to get to the
  other side!
George Washington never wore
  modern-day clothes.